We're All Characters

Good Boy Roy

We're All Characters: Good Boy Roy
Copyright © 2013

ISBN: 978-1-935256-29-8

BackDoor Books
PO Box 1652
Boone, NC 28607
(828) 263-9102
ledgepress.com
ledgepress@gmail.com

CRAZY TIMMY™

ZMAN™

Hippie Heather™

ANGRY ALLEN

ROCKER RICK

Soccer Chicks Rule!

MAXINE

Gooooo
TEAM

the GOOD BOY ROY dudes

ROY   HANDSOME HEN   CRAZY TIMMY   ROCKER RICK

THE GOOD MESSAGE RAPPER

BE TRUE
TO YOU!

GOOD BOY ROY: RAPSTAR

PEACE,
I'M OUT

STOP
THINK
THANK
RESPECT

BE COOL
BE GOOD

If you could be a Character, what would you be?

Draw it here and send it to Good Boy Roy and we will post it on our Facebook Page.
Send via e-mail attachment or mail to Good Boy Roy, 1 Brightleaf Ct, Simpsonville, SC 29680.

GOOD BOY ROY™
goodboyroy.com

www.ingramcontent.com/pod-product-compliance
Lightning Source LLC
Chambersburg PA
CBHW080939030426
42339CB00009B/482